15.00

8/1/17

WITHDRAWN

Electricity

Bulbs, Batteries, and Sparks

Written by Darlene R. Stille

Illustrated by Sheree Boyd

Special thanks to our advisers for their expertise:

Paul Ohmann, Ph.D., Assistant Professor of Physics
University of St. Thomas, St. Paul, Minnesota

Susan Kesselring, M.A., Literacy Educator
Rosemount-Apple Valley-Eagan (Minnesota) School District

PICTURE WINDOW BOOKS
MINNEAPOLIS, MINNESOTA

Managing Editor: Bob Temple
Creative Director: Terri Foley
Editor: Nadia Higgins
Editorial Adviser: Andrea Cascardi
Copy Editor: Laurie Kahn
Designer: John Moldstad
Page production: Picture Window Books
The illustrations in this book were prepared digitally.

Picture Window Books
1710 Roe Crest Drive
P.O. Box 669
North Mankato, MN 56003-0669
1-877-845-8392
www.capstonepub.com

Printed in the United States of America, North Mankato, Minnesota.
052012
006716R

Library of Congress Cataloging-in-Publication Data
Stille, Darlene R.
Electricity : bulbs, batteries, and sparks / written by Darlene Stille ;
illustrated by Sheree Boyd.
v. cm. — (Amazing science)
Includes bibliographical references and index.
Contents: An awesome force—What electricity can do—
How does electricity work?—Where does electricity come from?—
Electricity all around—Experiments—Play it safe around electricity.
ISBN 978-1-4048-0245-2 (hardcover)
ISBN 978-1-4048-0343-5 (softcover)
1. Electricity—Juvenile literature. [1. Electricity.]
I. Boyd, Sheree, ill. II. Title. III. Series.
QC527.2 .S76 2004
537—dc22

Table of Contents

An Awesome Force

Lightning flashes across the sky. It lights up storm clouds. The flash makes night as bright as day.

Lightning is a huge spark of electricity. The spark can jump between a cloud and the ground. It can jump from one cloud to another.

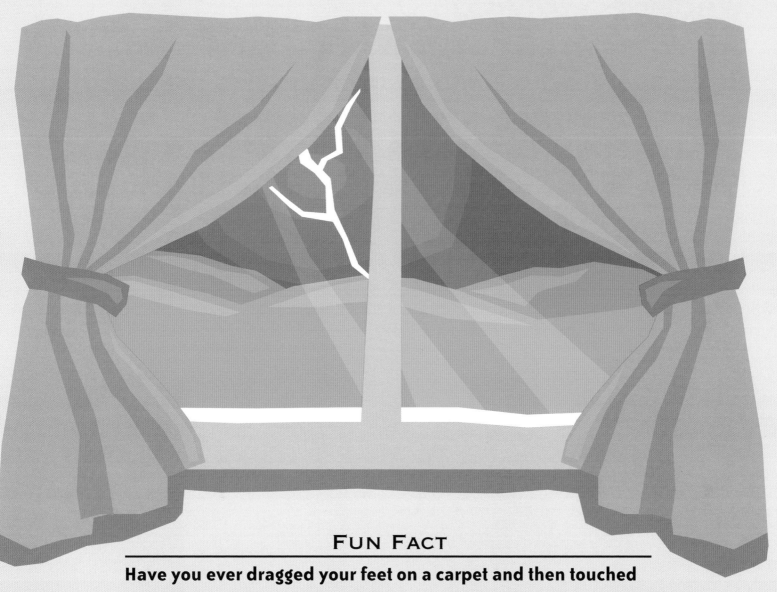

FUN FACT

Have you ever dragged your feet on a carpet and then touched a doorknob? The shock you felt in your fingers came from a kind of electricity called static electricity. Static electricity also makes lightning when ice and water rub against each other in a cloud.

What Electricity Can Do

Go into a dark room. Flick a switch on the wall. Electricity makes a lightbulb blink on, and the dark room becomes bright.

Electricity makes a toaster heat your bread. It makes the blades of a fan turn around and around. It makes the radio play.

FUN FACT

Anything that plugs in uses electricity. How many things in your home are powered by electricity?

7

How Does Electricity Work?

Electricity flows in an electric current, much like water flowing in a river. Electric current travels through wires in the walls of a house. The wires bring electricity to switches and outlets.

Plug in a vacuum cleaner. The electric current runs through the plug and up the cord into the vacuum cleaner's motor. Vrrroom!

Look at the cord on a hair dryer. It looks like it is made of rubber, but the rubber is only on the outside. There are metal wires inside the cord.

Electric current can go through only certain kinds of materials called conductors. Metal is the conductor that brings electricity from the outlet and through the cord.

FUN FACT

Electric current can't go through rubber easily. Rubber helps keep the electricity inside the wire. The rubber keeps you from getting a bad electric shock.

11

Look at the plug on a lamp. It has two prongs. Electricity goes from the outlet and into the lamp through one of the prongs. It goes from the lamp and back into the outlet through the other.

Around and around, electric current travels in a loop called a circuit.

FUN FACT

Some plugs have a third prong just below the other two. That prong isn't part of the electric circuit. It is a safety device. It helps send extra, dangerous electricity into the ground.

Push a button to turn off your TV. The button makes a gap in the circuit. The gap causes the electric current to stop. Press the button again. Closing the gap makes the current flow again.

14

Buttons, levers, and switches open
and close gaps in an electric circuit.
They make electric current stop and go.

15

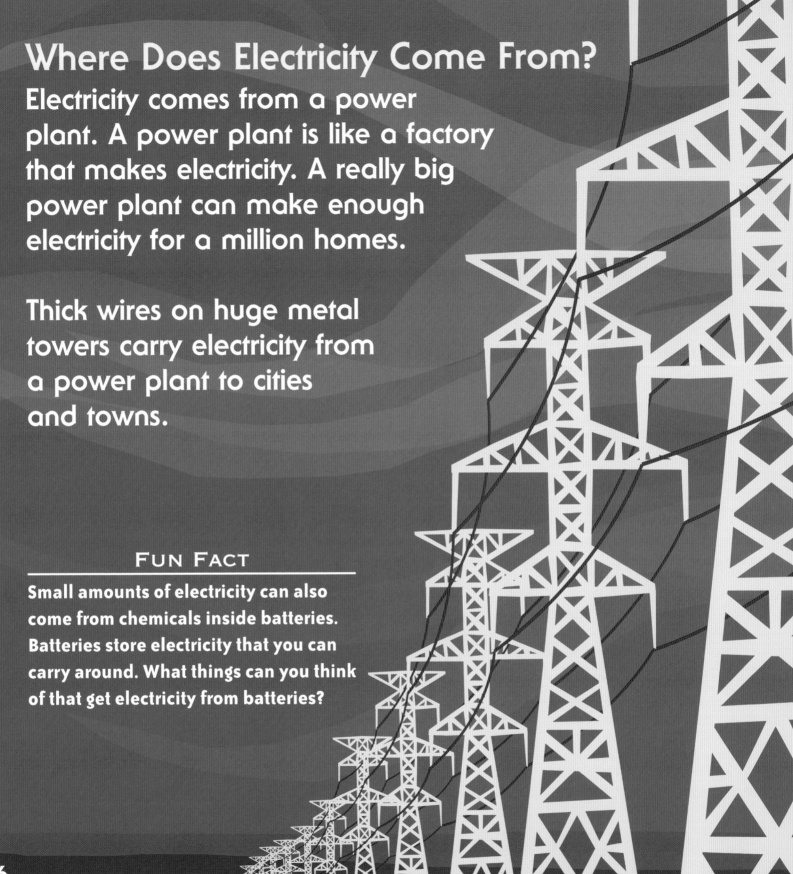

Where Does Electricity Come From?

Electricity comes from a power plant. A power plant is like a factory that makes electricity. A really big power plant can make enough electricity for a million homes.

Thick wires on huge metal towers carry electricity from a power plant to cities and towns.

FUN FACT

Small amounts of electricity can also come from chemicals inside batteries. Batteries store electricity that you can carry around. What things can you think of that get electricity from batteries?

16

Power plants need energy to make electricity. Most power plants get energy from burning coal, oil, or gas. Nuclear power plants get huge amounts of energy from a substance called uranium.

Some power plants get energy from falling water. Others use special windmills to make electricity.

FUN FACT

Solar cells turn sunlight into electricity. Solar cells make electricity for satellites in space.

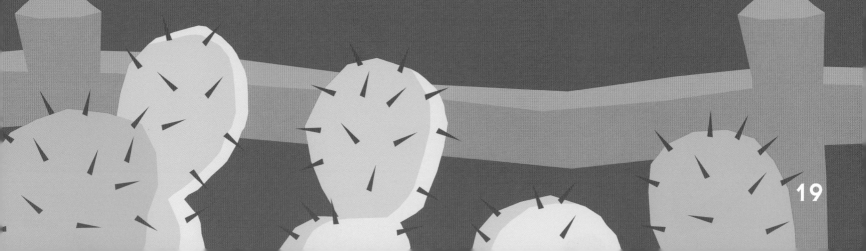

19

Electricity All Around

Some electricity comes from nature.
Some electricity is made by people.
Electricity is a powerful force.
You will find electricity
wherever you go.

FUN FACT

Electricity is even in your body. Your brain sends electric signals that tell your arms and legs to move. Electric signals tell your heart when to beat.

21

Experiments

Watch Static Electricity in Action

Blow up a balloon. Rub the balloon against your shirt. The rubbing makes static electricity. Hold the balloon against a wall. Take your hand away. What happens?

Rub the balloon against your shirt again. Now hold the balloon next to a friend's head. What hair-raising result did you get?

Watch an Electric Current in Action

What you need:
a flashlight battery (type C or D)
a thin piece of plastic-covered wire
    about 6 inches (15 centimeters) long
tape
a flashlight bulb

What you do:
1. Get an adult to help you.
2. Look at the battery carefully. Notice that the end with a bump on it has a plus sign. The flat end of the battery has a minus sign on it.
3. Have an adult help you take off about ½ inch (1 centimeter) of the plastic covering from each end of the wire.
4. Tape one end of the wire to the end of the battery that has the minus sign. Hold the bottom of the bulb against the end of the battery that has the plus sign. Have an adult touch the other end of the wire to the metal bottom of the bulb.

Does the bulb light up? You have made an electric circuit. An electric current is going through the circuit.

What happens when you take the wire away? You have made a gap in the circuit. Electricity cannot go through the gap. That is the way a switch works.

Play It Safe Around Electricity

Outdoors

Lightning is electricity and can be dangerous. It can start fires. It is powerful enough to hurt and even kill people. Stay indoors during a lightning storm. Don't stand near windows. Don't touch anything made of metal. Stay off the phone.

Power lines carry very strong electric currents. Never fly a kite near power lines. Your kite could get snagged in one. Electricity could then travel down your kite string and harm you.

Sometimes power lines blow down in a storm. If you see a power line on the ground, stay away! Tell an adult. Have them call 911 to get help right away.

Indoors

Never poke anything into an electrical outlet or appliance. Never use a knife or fork to get toast out of a toaster.

Unplug toasters, blenders, and other small kitchen appliances when you are not using them. Push the appliances to the back of the kitchen counter.

Be on the lookout for damaged electrical cords. If you see a damaged cord, tell an adult right away.

Electricity and water do not mix. Electricity can travel through water and hurt you. Never play a radio when you are in the shower or bathtub. Never use a hair dryer near water. Never stand in water and plug or unplug an electrical cord.

Glossary

conductor—a material, such as metal, that electricity can go through easily
electric circuit—a path that electricity flows through
electric current—a flow of electricity
power plant—a place that makes electricity for an entire city or region

To Learn More

At the Library
Cole, Joanna. *The Magic School Bus and the Electric Field Trip.* New York: Scholastic Press, 1997.
Dussling, Jennifer. *Lightning: It's Electrifying.* New York: Grosset & Dunlap, 2002.
Holderness, Jackie. *Why Does a Battery Make It Go?* Brookfield, Conn.: Copper Beech Books, 2002.
Olien, Rebecca. *Electricity.* Mankato, Minn.: Bridgestone Books, 2003.

On the Web
FactHound offers a safe, fun way to find Web sites related to topics in this book.
All of the sites on FactHound have been researched by our staff.

1. Visit *www.facthound.com*
2. Type in this special code: 1404802452
3. Click the FETCH IT button.

Your trusty Fact Hound will fetch the best sites for you!

Index